APOSTLE DANIEL AKPAI

THE ENGINE ROOM FOR GREATNESS

Email: pastordanakpai@gmail.com
Facebook: Apostle Daniel Akpai Ministries.
Phone: +234-812-433-4152

THE ENGINE ROOM FOR GREATNESS

DEDICATION

This book is dedicated first to the Almighty God for His help and inspiration through the manifestation of the Holy Spirit in my life.

ACKNOWLEDGMENT

I humbly acknowledge the strength behind my calling and ministry. The person of the sweet Holy Spirit.

I want to thank my Wife (Pst. Mrs Beauty Akpai) and to my two lovely Children (Lucia Owojo Akpai) and (AvielaUli-ejuojo Akpai).I love you all.....

CONTENTS

INTRODUCTION

One of the greatest desire of mankind is to attain greatness in life.

God is the GOD of order and principles, and greatness is one of our covenant heritage as GOD'S children. Unfortunately, you cannot access this greatness until you are fully endued with the secrets and prerequisites for greatness.

Judges 7:1-7

" Then Jerubbaal, who is Gideon and all the people that were with him, rose up early and pitched beside the well of Harod: so that the host of the Midianites were on the north side of them, by the hill of Moreh, in the valley".

"And the Lord said unto Gideon, the people that are with thee are too many for me

to give the Midianites into their hands, lest Israel vaunt themselves against me saying, mine own hand hath saved me.

"Now the therefore go to proclaim in the ears of the people, saying, whoso ever is

fearful and afraid, let him return and depart early from mount Gilead. And there returned of the people twenty and two thousand, and there remained ten thousand. And the Lord said unto Gideon, the people are yet too many...

Every professional or trained soldier desires many personnel to help him fight the enemies at any war but in this case God said the soldiers were too many. God knew many of those recruited for the battle were not prepared because, physical preparedness is never proportional to mental preparedness.

Greatness is not a place. Greatness is not a Man. There are things that give birth to greatness. Often times we pray and ask God, " Lord make me great, Lord give me this". It is good to pray for greatness but when the foundation of greatness is not in place , your prayer won't be answered and that is why God does not answer many people who prayed or wished for greatness. Greatness is not a wish, you don't wish to be great. Plenty soldiers were brought because a land needed to be conquered but some qualities were missing in them. God said these people were too many. God was not excited about the fight, He was not excited about the number, God was angry that they were plenty. I pondered WHY God detested the number of armies who volunteered to fight for a good course and I discovered majority of the armies lacked the prerequisites for greatness. The prerequisites were found in just three hundred (300) armies and thousands were relegated because they did not have all it takes to become great. READ FROM THE BEGINNING TILL THE END I TRUST GOD THAT YOU WILL FIND THE ENGINE ROOM THAT MAKES ONE GREAT.

CHAPTER ONE

Greatness Is Possible

Greatness has requirements and that is why it is impossible for you not to read this book because it will unveil this kingdom secrets to you. Ironically, only few have this kingdom prerequisites for greatness. Hear me; there is nobody that can not be great in life, there is no city that can't produce great people, there is no village that can't produce great people, there is no family that can't produce great children. The family of Jesse was one irrelevant and unrecognized family, they were neglected, rejected, nobody knew about this family, nobody recognized them because they were not influential, they were not powerful, they were not rich, they were not relevant, but something happened. God brought out somebody from that family and made him great, His name was David. I decided to study the life of David and in the course of my study, I discovered the secret to David's greatness, I will discuss that in the course of this book. No matter where you came from, no matter your background, no matter what people say about you, you can succeed if you mean it. The conclusion of men is never your final destination. I announce to somebody reading this and I declare that GOD is about to change your narratives. After my wedding in 2012, I waited and believed GOD for children for 5 years, what have we not heard? we have been called names, we have been mocked but by the 5th year, God turned our mockery into testimony today. I am a father of two lovely children, hear me Beloved, man cannot break what he didn't make therefore, you are God's representative here on earth and based on covenant heritage you are a carrier of greatness. I make a bold decree over your life that greatness will manifest in your life! Greatness will manifest in your life !! In Jesus name. You don't serve a a dead God, You serve a mighty God! He's the same yesterday, He's the same today, He's the same forever, When God says yes, no man can say No! When God lifts you up, no man can bring you down! God is on your side!

Greatness is on your side!

Everybody can be great, no matter where you came from. David was in the bush, greatness located him. Stop blaming your father for your financial state, if you look for who to blame you become lame. If you keep blaming your father your son will grow up to blame you too someday. It is important to note that your back is not on the ground because of your background it is because you never knew the engine room for greatness but thank GOD it shall be unveiled to you in this book.

Listen, when you complain, you Explain your PAIN for GAIN! Since you have been complaining what has it settled? I wish I came from the family of Dangote but Dangote came from an unknown family. Greatness can happen anywhere. It can happen in that your village . It can happen in that your family. I don't care what people say about you. Let them watch and see, before their eyes God will prove them wrong in Jesus mighty name.

There was a donkey tied in the village, the donkey was rejected, the donkey was neglected and Jesus said, "Go to the village against you then you will find a donkey, He said "Untie and bring it".

He said *"If the owner ask you tell them the master is in need of it"*. From study I found out that Prophet Zechariah prophesied about this donkey 500 years before CHRIST. God brought into fulfillment a prophecy given concerning an animal, at a point all hope was lost as the donkey kept seeing other donkies walking in glory with their masters but one thing was certain, the donkey was a carrier of prophecy. The moment Jesus came on the donkey the prophecy was fulfilled, you are a carrier of prophecy. The good news is that Jesus is not riding on us like he did in the donkey's case but he is living in us, GLORY!

You are meant to be great because you are a carrier of prophecy. You can't remain here, You can't die here.

You can't finish your assignment here.

There is a place called there! If there is a background, there's a future ground I know where I'm going.

The path of the just is like a shining light that shines more and more and more unto a perfect day. Say this after me, “I am not a failure, I don't care what I am going through, I have a seed of greatness, I can't end like this, yesterday was bad, today is better, tomorrow is the best". I'm writing to somebody like you. It can happen anywhere and greatness will happen to you!

When last did anyone try to identify with you? Nobody did that because you are yet to command some level of success. One of the signs that proved your greatness is when men begin to identify with you either publicly or secretly.

Isa.60:3

And the Gentiles shall come to thy light, and kings to the brightness of thy rising.

WHO ARE THE GENTILES?

From the scripture above we can either attract Gentiles or kings but what determines who we attract is what we manifest on the outside. If you walk in God's light alone you are only attracted to Gentiles. If we must understand the verse above we must first understand who the Gentiles are. See:

The Latin versions of the Bible translated goyim as gentiles (singular gens) or gentiles (an adjectival form of gens). In modern usage, “Gentile” applies to a single individual, although occasionally (as in English translations of the Bible) “the Gentiles” means “the nations.” In post biblical Hebrew, goy came to mean an individual non-Jew rather than a nation. Because most non-Jews in the Western world were Christians, Gentile came to be equated with Christian.

Strictly speaking however, any non-Jew is a Gentile. (Editor of Britannica)

Therefore, Gentiles are Christians who are non Jews since they are not biologically born Jews.

WHO ARE KINGS?

According to the Scripture the WORD KING is generally used to denote one invested with authority. This means that KINGS are those who have delegated authority to do things. Kingship speaks of those in power, those who have influence in the society; it speaks also of those who can bring you into limelight and relevance as themselves. You can never attract kings if you only demonstrate as light because the light alone brings the GENTILES. Only your rising can attract KINGS. Your rising speaks of your greatness; it speaks of your relevance.

Listen, you only attract your kind, the rich attracts the rich while the poor attracts the poor. Therefore your rising into greatness helps you to have a reshuffle of your existing friends and contacts. Forget what you see in Nollywood movies, where the rich marry the poor. Those scenes are fictional, they are not real, don't waste your time waiting for a billionaire that will come and change your life overnight. I am not saying that it is not possible. It is 100% possible but then such opportunity can only be potent when it meets a prepared person. This book is preparing you ahead.

"Greatness is achievable anywhere no matter where you come from" In fact, your background should provoke you to greatness.

Never blame your parents for your poor financial and material state. You are in that family to effect a change.

"A MAN'S GREATNESS LIES IN HIS POWER OF THOUGHT "(MIKE)

WE ARE ON PROBATION

Many of us who ask God for greatness are on probation.

Probation is a period where a new person that is employed is tested by character and ability.

Probation is a period where your employer tests your character before accepting you for the job. God is saying, "you want to be great, I have it in abundance, I will give you greatness but for now you are placed on probation, I want to watch you when you are broke, He wants to watch your attitude when you see God's little blessings in your life, He wants to know if you will still be committed to the church's weekly activities and He wants to know if you will still be humble enough to serve in that church's unit after seeing a few of His blessings.

When God places one on probation, He will open one small door for you and begin to monitor your character, commitment to HIM and many more. And one of the small doors that God opened was your university admission, job opportunity or financial breakthrough. Probation season! The season where many people who pray for greatness fail. Samson failed his probation test, king Saul failed his probation test too. One sad truth we don't know is that for every King Saul there is a hidden David and the worst that can happen to a person is to still remain on the throne meanwhile another has taken your crown. Whenever God blesses you with one little breakthrough, He begins to watch you.

You want to be known, you want to be heard as a voice, you want to be somebody people can watch on television, you have got so much mission, you have got so much dream, you have got so much idea, you know you can't fail, yet you failed your probation test, you won't have access to greatness. God cannot trust you if HE has not tested you.

I served God for fifteen years, prophesying, preaching on the altar. It is after fifteen years an angel appeared to me physically. God did not trust me for fourteen years. It was my probation period.

"Lord give me power, give me auction, give me wealth like Dangote" And the Lord says, Son, "I do not trust people any more.

My trust has been betrayed". If you want God to entrust you with so much greatness and relevance, you must be disciplined enough to pass His probation tests.

Do you know that Saul was not qualified to be king but God gave him to Israelites as their king but unfortunately, God's trust was betrayed.

God regretted choosing king Saul!

One of your prayer points on a daily basis should be, "Lord give me the grace not to misbehave in my probation period". Lord, don't regret for this privilege you have given me , give me the grace to keep the fire burning. We ask God for upliftment, we ask God for promotion, we ask God for next level and the next thing is, when God places you on probation, will you pass the test? GOD wants to watch you grow, HE is ready to place you on probation, HE wants to test your character and your reaction to things after HIS blessings.

You used to be an active member of a church before, you were even a worker in church but because of one open door, one small thing God did for you, you are now feeling on top of the world. Pride and arrogance has taken the place of God in your life. Things of God do not move you anymore. God says, ' I am watching you'. Those who misbehave with little blessings, are denied access to relevance and greatness.

How many of us knows the story of Joseph in the Bible? The Bible says he dreamt and in that dream, he saw the moon bowing, he saw the sun , stars and all of that. After that God placed him on probation, to see what he would do. He got to Potiphar's house, the woman came after him demanding for sex, that was still a probation period for him.

Probation is a period of test. God decided to test him with sex offered to him for free.

He said "I cannot do such a wickedness against my master" He passed that one then he was arrested and taken to the prison.

Probation! He was there, he interpreted a dream and the dream came to pass, so from the prison, he got to the palace . He did not become a prime minister by accident, he began when he succeeded in passing the exam of divine probation. Have you passed your own?

Lord you are testing me, help me not to fail, enlarge my heart.

There is one thing that God needs from a man if He must make you great. I will show you as we move further in this book.

"THE ENGINE ROOM FOR GREATNESS"

When you are on probation, some of the tests you see are;

When you are given a little money and you become too busy for church service, When you are given a job and you become busy for the things of God, you are saying "with the nature of my work, with the nature of my this"

God has placed you on probation. Some blessings you see are not actually the real blessings, they are just tests for the main blessings that are ahead!

When God wants to test you he will place you under people who will lead you as leaders. When you disrespect their hierarchy, you have failed. You will not fail your probation tests in Jesus name!

"IF YOU CHASE TWO RABBITS AT A TIME BOTH WILL ESCAPE" (JOHN MASON).

CHAPTER TWO

Greatness Is Not Luck

Greatness is not a function of luck. What makes great are God's favour, wisdom, personal revelation, hard work and obedience to covenant terms and principles.

Expecting greatness without the above mentioned ingredients is the biggest deception of all times, nothing works without someone working it out. Things that work have principles that make them work and in this chapter we shall be looking at some principles.

Solomon was the richest man ever lived; he was so great to a point where he became envy to his world. Queen of Sheba heard and visited King Solomon because his fame spread abroad. Beloved, people don't identify with unsuccessful people but my desire for you is that after reading this book and putting to work what you would learn, you shall experience greatness in Jesus name!

It is important to note that if you must have access

to kingdom greatness you must be fully born again. We have two types of births:

1. Natural birth
2. Spiritual birth

Everyone on earth once experienced natural birth through the biological parents; kingdom greatness doesn't begin at natural birth it begins at spiritual birth. Spiritual birth is the process of regeneration from the old you to the new you through the blood of Jesus by confessing that Jesus is the Son of God, believing in your heart as well as denouncing your sins and turning away from the old lifestyle.

"For whatsoever is born of God overcometh the world: and this is the victory ***that overcometh the world, even our faith." 1 John 5:4***

"But as many as received him, to them gave he power to become the sons of God, even to them that believe on his name:"

John 1:12

"For as much then as the children are partakers of flesh

and blood, he also himself likewise took part of the same; that through death he might destroy him that had the power of death, that is, the devil;" Hebrews 2:14

Your new birth is not only the gateway to heaven, it is also your access to kingdom greatness.

From the day you became born again, you become a partaker of kingdom greatness by covenant. What works in God is now operational in you.

"But as it is written, Eye hath not seen, nor ear heard, neither have entered into the heart of man, the things which God hath prepared for them that love him. But God hath revealed them unto us by his Spirit: for the Spirit searcheth all things, yea, the deep things of God. For what man knoweth the things of a man, save the spirit of man which is in him? even so the things of God knoweth no man, but the Spirit of God." 1 Corinthians 2:9-11,

Your greatness is predestined; you are not to be intimidated by the achievement of any. You see, in life some people must arrive before you but at times GOD allows people to arrive before you so they can welcome you on your day of arrival. There are great and mighty things that God is set to do through you. No human eyes have seen it, no heart has conceived it, no mind has imagined it. many years ago I remember when I fasted without food, I remember when I had no shoes. There was even a time a lady turned down my marriage proposal because I was very broke but today God is glorified. Only the mocked can be made. Personally, I have discovered that at times God stays off from the scenario of our issues to see our reaction and to as well allow men to have a say before His final intervention.

TO BE ABLE TO ACHIEVE KINGDOM GREATNESS, YOU MUST DISCOVER YOUR POTENTIAL.

Your potency is divinely connected to your potential. Your impact is highly proportional to your potential. So, to be able to effect your greatness in this kingdom your potential must be discovered.

Potential is the ability to develop into something

in the future. In other words, potential is the latent abilities that may be developed and lead to future success or usefulness.

It is important to know that every child of God has got a potential that is meant to bring him greatness and relevance in life.

Prov. 18:16

A man's gift makes room for him
and brings him before the great
Men

HOW CAN I DISCOVER MY POTENTIAL?

Since one's potential is one of the things needed for kingdom greatness. It becomes important for every covenant child of God to discover it deliberately. Passion is a great pointer to unveiling your potential.

1. Passion: Your potential lies in what you are passionate for. Whatever you love doing even without being paid is your potential.

Ironically, whatever you can't do for free today you won't be paid for it tomorrow. If you are passionate for something and you are given an opportunity to serve with it, kindly serve humanity with it even if it is for free the reason is that, when you are given the opportunity to serve, it is another privilege given to you to nurture your potential into something big in future. Never feel you are being used. Hear this; if men can't use you God won't use you.

Elisha left everything he had to follow his master (Elijah), Elisha was called all manner of names following and serving his master. The sons of the prophet even mocked Elisha when he was about to be taken by the chariot of fire, they mocked him as though the person he spent all his life serving was going to leave him without any compensation meanwhile the reward of passion was a mile away from him. Elisha who passionately served his master later got the double portion of Elijah, he recorded twice the miracles of his master.

Elisha, unlike his master (Elijah) related with kings and the most influential people of his time. Passion brought him into relevance and greatness, he would have ended like any other farmer in town but passion changed the narratives. You can change your family's pattern, you can change the general belief system in your entire village, you can make it, if you mean it. I have preached without honorarium, I have fasted and prayed for people without requesting anything from anyone even till date, I have spent millions on church projects without using the money for my personal needs, I have given cars and other material things to the work of the ministry without any form of regrets. Do you know what has been driving me? PASSION!

Psalm 69:9

The passion for your house has consumed me...

Get back to your potential and become passionate for it. Be resolute and committed to it, in the end it will pay.

THINGS YOU CAN DO TO EFFECT YOUR POTENTIAL

Factor Of Love; You Must Love Your Assignment.

"He that hath my commandments, and keepeth them, he it is that loveth me: and he that loveth me shall be loved of my Father, and I will love him, and will manifest myself

to him." John 14:21

2. You must be humble; It takes humility to receive instruction from God.

3. Obedience to divine leading ***"His mother saith unto the servants, Whatsoever he saith unto you, do it."*** John2:5
4. Consistency and focus

Covenant practice of giving to God and the poor

SUPERNATURAL WISDOM OF GOD, ANOTHER PREREQUISITE FOR GREATNESS.

King Solomon was the richest man ever lived on earth. During his reign gold and silver were common in the land; his reign was full of peace and tranquility unlike the reign of his father (David). I personally studied the life of Solomon and all I saw was a man full of supernatural wisdom, fortunately his GREATNESS was birthed by the supernatural wisdom that was bestowed on him by God.

2 Chro.1:7-11

That night God appeared to Solomon and said to him, "Ask for whatever you want me to give you."

Solomon answered God, "You have shown great kindness to

David my father and have made me king in his place.

Now, LORD God, let your promise to my father David be confirmed, for you have made me king over a people who are as numerous as the dust of the earth.

Give me wisdom and knowledge, that I may lead this people, for who is able to govern this great people of yours?"

God said to Solomon, "Since this is your heart's desire and you have not asked for wealth, possessions or honor, nor for the death of your enemies, and since you have not asked for a long life but for wisdom and knowledge to govern my people over whom I have made you king."Happy is the man that findeth wisdom, and the man that getteth understanding. For the merchandise of it is better than the merchandise of silver, and the gain thereof than fine gold. She is more precious than rubies: and all the things thou canst desire are not to be

compared unto her. Length of days is in her right hand; and in her left hand riches and honour. Her ways are ways of pleasantness, and all her paths are peace. "She is a tree of life to them that lay hold upon her: and happy is every one that retaineth her. The LORD by wisdom hath founded the earth; by understanding hath he established the heavens." Proverb 3:13-19, "And when the sabbath day was come, he began to teach in the synagogue: and many hearing him were astonished, saying,

From whence hath this man these things? And what wisdom is this which is given unto him, that even such mighty works are wrought *wealth you give him he will still return to poverty. Financial, marital and material management lies in supernatural wisdom.* ***"Receive, I pray thee, the law from his mouth, and lay up his words in thine heart.***

If thou return to the Almighty, thou shalt be built up, thou shalt put away iniquity far from thy tabernacles. Then shalt thou

lay up gold as dust, and the gold of Ophir as the stones of the brooks. Yea, the Almighty shall be thy defence, and thou shalt have plenty of silver."

Job 22:22-25

May the Lord give you supernatural wisdom for kingdom greatness in Jesus name.

"POVERTY IS A DISEASE OF THE MIND" (S.B FULLER)

CHAPTER THREE

The Engine Room For Greatness

Like I stated earlier in the previous chapters, greatness is one of the major things we have as our inheritance but the problem is, how do I flow in kingdom greatness ? How do I access kingdom greatness ? What is the major prerequisite for kingdom greatness ? The major answer will be found in this chapter.

Acts 13:22

"After removing Saul, he made David the king. He testified concerning him. I have found David son of Jesse a man after my own heart, he will do everything I want him to do".

First and foremost we need to know why God called David a man after his own heart. See the reason below.

Psalm 51:10

Create in me a clean heart, oh

God, and renew a right spirit within me.

Can you see why God testified of David's heart? can you see why God called him a man after his own heart ? It's because David knew that the only thing that makes one great in this kingdom is the **HEART**. the major engine room for greatness is the **HEART**. It determines the motives behind your quest and desire for money, fame, wealth, relevance and any other thing that makes one feel fulfilled. Your motive is one of the determinants of your prayers and requests.

Ironically, if your heart is good alongside your motive, you will definitely have access to so many great things in life without praying or fasting for them. A good and Godly heart is attractive to good and great things. God out of his infinite mercy can give things to some persons with bad hearts but i can boldly tell you that such people don't tend to last in the blessings of God because whatever God's mercy gives, one's character can destroy it if not worked upon.

Let us look at what happened to King Saul quickly.

1Sam. 16:1

The lord said to Samuel, "How

long will you mourn for Saul, since i have rejected him as king over Israel? Fill your horn with oil and be on your way, i am sending you to Jesse of Bethlehem. I have chosen one of his sons to be king.

King Saul, the anointed king was rejected by the same God that approved him. By privilege, he was the first king in Israel but because of the matter of the heart he disobeyed divine instruction and lost his throne to David. David as young as he was, was very smart to know the pitfall of his predecessor Saul, he knew Saul missed it because of heart problem. Your heart determines what comes to your hands. David was smart to pray to God to create and renew his heart and his spirit.

The secret of Joseph's greatness in Egypt was the heart. If your heart is good, let the whole world gather together against you, they will fail while you prevail.

1Peter 3:3

And who is he that will harm you, if you be followers of that which is good?.

A man with a good heart enjoys divine immunity.

The gathering of the wicked is never a threat because God does not even see anything as a threat from the enemies, hallelujah! Because Joseph was a young man who had a good heart, look at what he did.

Gen. 39:9

There is none greater in this house than i, neither hath he kept back anything from me but thee, because thou art his wife, how then can I do this great wickedness, and sin against God ?

Joseph was lifted above many in portiphar's house in addition; Joseph was a tall handsome and good looking young man. His master's wife came and requested for sex one faithful day when his master was not around but because Joseph's heart was good he was able to resist mouth watering temptation that was presented to him for free. If you will forget anything in this book please don't forget this, "what you lose when you sin is greater than what you gain when you sin". No matter how cheap a sin may be, its consequences are damaging. God forgives sins but the sinners must face the consequences of their sins. Secondly, God forgives sins but people don't forget it, I hope you can see the tragedy of sins already. I had a fellowship member who was a womanizer back then in our fellowship, he later met with the Lord and became born again in our fellowship but before then he was never serious with his studies, so when he got born again there were plenty carry overs waiting for him. God forgave him the sins but he faced the consequences of his sin by not getting a certificate after his graduation because of too many carry overs.

Can you see why you must run from sin?

Before I forget, there is this story of a young girl I can never forget, while I was on campus, the sister met me and told me she came from a poor family and that she did prostitution from her first year to her last year to sponsor herself in the university, when she met me she was already in her final year and was tested positive of HIV virus. She met me crying and telling me how ready she was to get born again, I led her to Christ and her sins were forgiven but this sister later died even after her repentance. Why didn't you pray for her to get healed pastor? I did but the Lord still called her home. Can you see the consequence of sin? One big thing you need to know about the devil and sin is that when the devil advertises sins to you, he won't present it to you with its consequences; he presents only the temporal pleasure. Receive grace for purity in Jesus name!

CHAPTER FOUR

The Covenant Of Greatness

We can't discuss greatness without considering God's covenant for greatness. Greatness is one of the covenant rights we have as children of the kingdom. Let's look at the concept of covenant. According to the Latin origin, the word "covenant" is called (con venire) which means "to come together".

It therefore means that a covenant is simply the coming together of two or more persons to make a contract, agreeing on promises, stipulation, privileges and responsibilities. In Old Testament the word covenant appeared about 280 times and it was used in New Testament for 33 times.

Biblically, a covenant is a legal agreement between two or more persons sealed with an oath enforced with terms and conditions. This means that no covenant person can enjoy the blessings of God's covenant until the both parties keep to the terms and conditions of the covenant initiated. Let's look at the covenants of God's salvation to humanity.

John 3:16-18

For God so love the world, that he gave his only begotten son,that whosoever believe in him should not perish but have everlasting life.

***For God sent not his son into the world to condemn the world; but that the world through him might be saved He that believeth on him is not condemned: but he that believeth not is condemned already, because he hath not** believed in the name of the only begotten son of God.*

God's only purpose for sacrificing His begotten son is to save man from sin that was committed by the first Adam at the Garden of Eden. God gave his son to save humanity but there are hidden terms or conditions embedded in "***vs. 16"*** as quoted above.

.... that whosoever believeth in him...

John 3:16. God has initiated a saving covenant for humanity but this covenant of salvation can only be obtained by those who keep to the terms and conditions of the covenant. The covenant terms and conditions for our salvation is BELIEVING IN JESUS; anyone who doesn't believe in Jesus cannot enjoy the gift of salvation that has been given to us. So, salvation is free but it has its terms and conditions for it to add value in our lives.

See John 3:18b

....but he that believeth not is condemned already, because he has not believed in the name of the only begotten son of God.

Believing Jesus gives us access to the saving power of Jesus blood which was shed on the cross of Calvary.

ACTIVATING THE COVENANT OF GREATNESS.

These are prerequisites that give us access to easy and stable flow of God's covenant blessings and in this chapter I will be exposing us to things that can give us full access to covenant greatness.

THE COVENANT TERMS OR

CONDITIONS FOR GREATNESS.

(1). Be a seeker of God's kingdom.

Mat. 6:33

But seek ye first the kingdom of God, and his righteousness, and all these things shall be added unto you.

A believer who seeks God can't lack anything good in life. Everything you are praying for are all kept in God's kingdom for you, that is why when Jesus taught his disciples how to pray he personally taught them his way.

Mat. 6:9-10

This, then, is how you should pray: "Our father in heaven, hallowed be your name, your kingdom come, your will be done, on earth as it is in heaven.

Jesus knew that everything we need in life are kept in God's kingdom for us, so praying and asking God to release His kingdom to us is the same as bringing God's divine supplies to ourselves.

So, when we seek his kingdom everything people

die to get will supernaturally come to us. A kingdom seeker goes after lost souls, he is committed to God in his or her local church in a church unit. A seeker of his kingdom won't quit a church or unit because someone insulted him or her. Paul said, “what can separate me from the love of Christ?”

I remembered when I had one particular motorcycle in 2004; I traveled from village to village preaching the gospel to the unreached villagers, in many instances our lives were threatened by hoodlums and bad guys who were angry with us because of the gospel we brought to them. I remember one particular night we had a rural crusade in one village. It was very cold that night that we had to go to the generator to get ourselves warm because of the level of cold that night. I remember moving from street to street doing morning cry in the city of Port Harcourt in 2009. Have I relented? the answer is No! we have intensified our soul winning strategies and weekly, we ensure we reach out to dying souls, this is what it means to seek God's kingdom. You can't have a share of the kingdom until you are first a kingdom seeker **(2). You must do something:** There is no great idle person. Every great person has something doing. Let's check the lives of bible characters who were covenant people, who did excellently well in the bible. Abraham was a herdsman; Isaac was a farmer and herdsman while Jacob was a well digger. Can't you see that these covenant men were able to achieve greatness by doing something? No lazy person has a place in this covenant except if he/she is ready to work out of laziness.

2Thess. 3:10

For even when we were with you, we gave you this rule: "The one who is unwilling to work shall not eat".

The line has to be drawn because many Christian are becoming lazy in the name of faith, remember;

James 2:14

What does it profit, my brethren, if someone says he has faith but does not have works? can faith save him?

Faith does not tell you to stop working; it rather encourages us to work. God does not prosper nothing or vacuum but he prospers something. see

Psalm 1:3

And he shall be like a tree planted by the rivers of water, that bringeth forth his fruit in his season, his leaf also shall not wither, and what so ever he doeth shall prosper *This covenant of prosperity of work has no regard for your location, color and career.*

This covenant cuts across borders, you can succeed anywhere if you do something and keep to all covenant terms of greatness. Until you keep to all terms and conditions, you can be hard working and still die poor. Hear this, hard work does not make man great, only covenant principles makes great and if you doubt it then, check your neighborhood, you will find water vendors (Mai-Ruwa) who work so hard daily selling water but none has emerged a millionaire. Last year alone God opened my eyes to a business that gave me about #12million in less than 12 months.

Look, there is legitimate wealth in your country, state or local government where you are. If only you can keep to your own terms and conditions of covenant as discussed in this chapter then you are on your way to an unending flow of financial prosperity and kingdom greatness.

(3). The term of tithe and offering: This is the most interesting part that has changed my life for good. I got born again in 2003 but, I understood tithing when I joined Winners Chapel in 2005. I have been practicing from then till 2015 when I stepped up my tithing from 10% to 15% and 20%. In this aspect I will personally pour out my heart to you how God delivered me from financial struggles and crises as a believer.

WHAT IS A TITHE?

A tithe is one-tenth part of something or money given to your church daily, weekly or yearly. Just the way God takes our 10% as tithe, the government takes its part as Tax too. The government takes tax from its citizens to generate revenue that can fund the projects such as social amenities, pay salaries etc.

Mal. 3:10

Bring ye all the tithes into the store house, that there may be meat in mine house, and prove me now herewith, said the Lord of hosts, if i will not open you the windows of heaven, and pour you out a blessing, that there shall not be room enough to receive it.

The word tithing has become a bone of contention among many grace preachers, many of them are of the opinion that tithing is an act of the law and that the law is no longer effective in New Testament because of what Jesus did on the cross. The fact is that tithing is never an act of the law; it is an act of FAITH.

Let's look at where tithe was first mentioned in the scripture.

Gen. 14:19-20

And he blessed Abram and said: "Blessed be Abram by God most high, creator of heaven and the earth, and blessed be God most high, who has delivered your enemies into your hands". Then Abram gave Melchizedek a tenth (tithe) of everything.

The scripture above is the first time the word tithe was mentioned in the bible, the question now is, was the law given by Moses as at when tithe was given? the answer is capital NO ! In fact nobody knew the grandfather of Moses (the law giver) as at that time because, they were not born when Abraham first gave his tithe talk more of Moses the law giver.

WHY DID ABRAHAM TITHE?

(a). **Abraham tithed in appreciation to God for the victory over his enemies** - you give your tithe in appreciation to God over your daily, weekly and yearly victories. It's not everyone that makes profits from what they do, some lost, but God gave you profit because of his covenant in your life. You give your tithe from your salary because it is not everyone who applied for the same job was able to get it; you give your tithe in appreciation to God for giving you the job opportunity.

(b). **Abraham tithed by faith**: Abraham is known as a man of faith and almost everything Abraham did were acts of faith, except some of his pitfalls. Abraham who never met Melchizedek prior to that time believed that he was reincarnate of Jesus.

Heb. 7:11

If therefore perfection were by the Levitical priest hood, (for under it the people received the law), what further need was there that another priest should rise after melchizedek and not be called after the order of Aaron.

By faith Abraham believed and gave his tithe to

Jesus reincarnate. Till date tithing is an act of faith in God for more supplies and kingdom blessings.

(c). **Abraham gave his tithe as an act of worship**: We give our tithe to God as an expression of reverence and adoration to God.

Before you bow to the fleshy contention of not giving your tithe, kindly ask yourself this question:

- If I gave my whole life to Christ why can't I give my 10% to God?

- If it was not too big for God to give to me why should my tithe be too big to give to God?

- Is it a sin to give back to God what He gave to me in the first place?

- Has the last tithe I kept to myself made me rich?

You can see that the list goes on and on if we want to ask questions.

THE BENEFIT OF TITHING.

Giving your tithe to God opens you up to supernatural blessings. Tithing is another covenant terms and conditions that opens you up to God's covenant of greatness on the end time church. Someone is asking questions, are all these billionaires tithers? and if they are not tithers, how do they manage to get so rich in money and material things? The answer is simple, we are all aware that God gives prosperity but do you know that the devil has devilishly replicated God by giving out wealth and prosperity too?

Prov. 10:22

The blessing of the Lord brings wealth and adds no sorrow with it.

From the verse above is it clear that apart from Godly prosperity there is another source of prosperity that comes with sorrow?

So, it is wrong to compare God's system of prosperity to that of the world's system of prosperity. Those who are desperate of getting money from the devil can go as far as killing their loved ones for money or selling their souls. The devil gives them some certain terms and conditions before giving them his temporary wealth. As for us (God's children) the only way to have access to kingdom's prosperity is by keeping to the terms and conditions of the covenants given to us by God.

As part of our covenant terms and conditions for covenant greatness, we must get use to giving to the Lord and helping the poor.

Phil.4

"The blessing of the Lord brings wealth and adds no sorrow with it". (Prov. 10 : 22)

CHAPTER FIVE

The Anointing, Another Factor For Greatness

Zechariah 4:6

Then he answered and spake unto me, saying, "this is the word of the Lord unto Zerubbabel, saying, not by might (or army) nor by power, but BY MY SPIRIT , saith the lord of hosts.

The anointing is not the oil; the anointing is the Holy Spirit.

Acts 10:38

How God anointed Jesus of Nazareth with the Holy Ghost and power, who went about doing good, and healing all that were oppressed of the devil, for God was with him.

Jesus was not anointed with oil, he was anointed with the Holy Spirit which was backed by power for signs, wonders and greatness.

WHAT DOES IT MEAN TO BE ANOINTED IN THE OLD TESTAMENT?

It is the act of pouring aromatic oil over an individual's body or head, but looking at the biblical verse under this topic, it is clear that Jesus in the later covenant was not anointed with physical oil; he was anointed with the Holy Spirit (Ghost).

In Old Testament what happened when David was anointed?

1 Samuel 16:13

So Samuel took the horn of oil and anointed him in the presence of his brothers, and from that day on, THE SPIRIT OF THE LORD came powerfully upon David. Samuel then went to Ramah.

In Old Testament it was ceremonial oil that was poured on people by the prophets or priests that made the spirit of God resident in them. Great characters of the bible at a point in their lives experienced the pouring of the anointing over them by higher spiritual persons. In New

Testament we receive the anointing (the Holy Spirit) at new birth (when we got born again).

1 John 2:27

As for you, the anointing you received from him remains in you, and you do not need anyone to teach you. But as his anointing teaches you about all things and as that anointing is real, not counterfeit - just as it has taught you, remain in him.

The scripture above shows how full we are with the anointing of God manifested as the Holy Spirit in us beginning from the day we became born again.

The anointing which has been given to us is here to teach us all things, including the secret keys to kingdom greatness. Greatness has secrets, only the anointing (Holy Spirit) can teach us those deep secrets.

John 14:24

But the advocate, the Holy Spirit, whom the father will send in my name, will teach you all things and will remind you of everything I have said to you.

The anointing is a teaching anointing. The Holy Spirit is here to teach and to remind us the things we need to do to access greatness of the kingdom. Jesus speaking:

John 14:12

'And greater works than these shall he do."

The Holy Spirit (Anointing) has been giving to us to do greater works, it has been given to you to do what nobody has done in your whole family. A great shift happened the day you got born again, there was a regeneration of another you. You can't fail carrying the heavy presence of this Holy Spirit. Battles are real but what is more real is the power of God.

WHY DO YOU NEED THE ANOINTING?

Greatness is not automatic, anything that works has its working principles that makes it work, the Holy Spirit (anointing) teaches you the principles that helps you in accessing greatness and secondly, the anointing empowers us for the battles for greatness.

Every great destiny has many evil powers to

contend with.

1 Cor, 16; 9

For a great door and effectual is opened unto me, and there are many adversaries. *There are forces to contend with, there are adversaries to fight if you must manifest your greatness in full.*

Over 15 years ago I had an experience I can never forget; there were this thugs in the town (Anyigba) a place in Kogi State, Nigeria. These guys were known everywhere as thugs in fact, no police could make any arrest in that part of the town where they lived. So many times they would hijack me and beg for money, I can't remember any particular day I have not given them money because you can't escape them without giving them money if they hijack your car.

THE UNEXPECTED HAPPENED

One faithful day, I was with one of my workers, then my fellowship takes place at my father's compound and suddenly I saw these thugs coming with anger and violence with all manner of weapons - when I rose my head up from where I sat to look carefully, I saw the guy who led them pointing towards our compound, the same thugs who I used to give money had already surrounded me and my worker who was with me that day. I saw heavy arms with these fellows as they were already threatening to first remove my two eye balls before attacking my life. It was full of terror as we stood looking up only unto God. When they got to where I was, they shouted and asked "where is the man of God?" At that point, the anointing (Holy Spirit) whispered to me saying “Now leave their midst and go to another different place and watch". I quickly left them while they were looking at me in confusion and later stood somewhere looking at how the event would unfold, I was there when they started fighting each other.

Guess what the spirit of the Lord did, the spirit of the Lord changed my identity because I was transformed into another man physically. The same people who begged me for money could not identify me anymore.

Isa, 59:19

So shall they fear the name of the Lord from the west and his glory from the rising of the sun. When the enemy shall come in

like a flood, the spirit of the lord shall lift up a standard against him.

The spirit of the lord did rose a standard against them, God personally confused them and gave me victory. It was after the event I discovered that a pastor who had a ministry close to my fellowship venue was the one who fornicated with the girlfriend of one of them, so they decided to finish the pastor that day, meanwhile I was mistaken for the pastor since the boyfriend of the girl didn't know the pastor in person. I would have been killed in place of another man's sin without the anointing, I would have been destroyed without the anointing but the anointing set me free to see the fullness of kingdom greatness in my life and ministry. Today all those thugs who came to kill me are all dead.

None is alive among them, the anointing that preserves also destroys.

Isa, 10:27

In that day their burden will be lifted from your shoulder, then yoke from your neck; the yoke will be DESTROYED because of the anointing.

You need the anointing to flow in kingdom greatness; you need the anointing to see cheap victories over powers that contend with your greatness, you also need the anointing to experience longetivity.

THE NECESSITY FOR THE ANOINTING.

Luke 24:29

And behold. I send the promise of my father upon you; but tarry ye in the city of Jerusalem until ye be endued with power from on high.

The book of acts of apostles is an encyclopedia of the move of God through the early apostles and from my personal study and research, I discovered that the move of God was triggered by the encounter they had with divinity at upper room. The Holy Spirit visited the house. They were launched into the deepest part of God via the anointing that fell at upper room.

HOW SOLOMON BECAME GREAT VIA THE ANOINTING

We know how Solomon came into the family of

his father (David). Solomon by human qualifications was not qualified to ascend to the throne of his father because of the illegality that happened between his father and his mother (Bathsheba). Let's see how Bathsheba became David's wife.

2samuel 11:1-15

In the spring, at the time when kings go off to war, David sent Joab out with the king's men and the whole Israelites army.

They destroyed the ammonites and besieged Rabbah. But David remained in Jerusalem.

One evening David got up from his bed and walk around on the roof of the palace.

from the roof he saw a woman bathing.

The woman was very beautiful.

And David sent someone to find out about her. The man said "she is Bathsheba, the daughter of Eliam and the wife of Uriah the Hittite".

Then David sent a messenger to

get her, she came to him and he slept with her. (Now she was purifying herself from her monthly uncleanness). Then she went back home.

The woman conceived and sent word to David, saying "I am pregnant".

So David sent his word to Joab"send me Uriah the Hittite". And Joab sent him to David.

When Uriah came to him, David asked how Joab was, how the soldiers were and how the war was going.

Then David said to Uriah, "go down to your house and wash your feet". So Uriah left the palace, and a gift from the king was sent after him.

Vs 14: In the morning David wrote a letter to Joab and sent it through Uriah.

15. In it he wrote, "put Uriah out in from where the fighting is fiercest, then withdraw from him so he will be struck down and die".

After the death of Uriah, David inherited his wife, because of the anger of God against David and his evil act God killed the baby Bathsheba was pregnant of, until they later gave birth to Solomon. Prior to this time David had sons who were meant to be the heir to David's throne especially Amnon his first son. See *1chronicle 3:1-2* but unfortunately Amnon was killed by Absalom when he raped his sister Jammar.

According to the Jewish tradition Absalom who became the first born was meant to be king in his father's stead.

LOOK AT WHAT THE ANOINTING DID

1 Kings 1:34

There have Zadok the priest and Nathan the prophet anoints him king over Israel. Blow the trumpet and shout, long live king Solomon.

Against the battles from Adonijah, Solomon emerged the king of Israel. Power was handed over to him (Solomon) via the anointing. Ironically, Solomon was the first king who got double anointing upon him to the throne.

He was anointed with corporate anointing from Nathan (the prophet) and Zadok (the priest).

The prophet operates as a messenger of God who takes message from God to the people while the priest is an advocate who takes people's message to God as the representative of the people. The double anointing was the reason why Solomon could function as a prophet, king and as well advocate on behalf of the people.

SOLOMON THE RICHEST KING EVER LIVED

Because of the anointing, Solomon remain the richest king ever lived and Solomon reigned for forty (40) years.

Solomon, according to research, made 25 tons of gold annually and if that is calculated by today's prices in dollars then each tons of gold cost about $2,000 which is about $70,000,000 per ton of gold. This therefore means that Solomon made about $2 trillion from gold alone apart from his other sources of income. Can you see what the anointing can do in one's life? Do you know the New Testament anointing which we received at new birth can make you greater than Solomon?

ANOTHER KIND OF THE ANOINTING.

I can't write about the anointing without mentioning the role of anointing oil in our Christian faith. In as much as we have the anointing as God's spirit in us, the scripture has admonished us to also use the anointing oil to minister to the sick if the need arises.

James 5:14-15

Is any sick among you? let him call for the elders of the church and let them pray over him, anointing him with oil in the name of the Lord : And the prayer of faith shall save the sick, and the Lord shall raise him up, and if he has committed sins, they shall be forgiven.

This therefore means that the fact that we carry the anointing (Holy Spirit) in us does not mean we shouldn't use the anointing oil - The anointing oil is a medium through which God's supernatural power is demonstrated.

DELIVERED FROM DEATH.

One early morning my younger sister and some

persons rushed one sister to my residence in Abuja. Though I don't see people for prayers and counseling in my house, I do that in church but because she is my immediate younger sister I defered that protocol to quickly attend to the situation. Opening the door I saw a lady that was carried almost lifeless, I asked what happened, they told me she screamed from her sleep and became paralyzed from her legs to the spinal cord. While she was lying in the parlor she became more lifeless as we looked at this lady going in our very eyes, I prayed nothing happened then I was led to anoint her with anointing oil in my house, after anointing her, she started walking and talking to the glory of God. Today she is still alive.

Anointing destroys yokes. You are anointed for greatness . Hallelujah!

"HONESTY IS THE FIRST CHAPTER OF THE BOOK OF WISDOM" (JOHN MASON)

HOW TO ACTIVATE THE ANOINTING OF THE HOLY SPIRIT IN US.

1. Repent from your sin and any form of ungodliness.
2. Accept Jesus as your personal Lord and savior.
3. Go for the knowledge of God's word through consistent study of the bible
4. Acknowledge the presence of the Holy Spirit in you.

May you enjoy the anointing in full henceforth!

God bless you…

www.ingramcontent.com/pod-product-compliance
Lightning Source LLC
LaVergne TN
LVHW050342160826
845677LV00014B/3747

9798847700801